Sister Rules

144 WAYS TO BE
A GOOD SISTER

ELIZABETH KILLMAN RUSSO

The information contained in this book is based upon the personal experiences of the author. It is not intended as a substitute for consulting with your parents or therapist. Any attempt to break one of the rules herein is done at your own peril.

The publisher does not advocate adherence to any particular rule, but believes the advice in this book should be available to sisters everywhere. The publisher and author are not responsible for any adverse consequences resulting from any of the suggestions discussed in this book (unless they turn out positive). Should the reader have any questions concerning the appropriateness of any rule mentioned, the authors and the publisher strongly suggest consulting with your sister(s) before you try to break one.

Published by:
The Book Couple LLC
Boca Raton, FL • www.thebookcouple.com

ISBN: 978-0-9908458-1-2

Illustration of Heart Sisters: Elizabeth Russo
Editing & cover design: Carol Killman Rosenberg
Interior design: Gary A. Rosenberg

Printed in the United States of America

For my daughters, Megan, Kaitlyn, and Kristen.
Thank you for the inspiration.

For the sisters God blessed me with at birth,
the sisters God sent me along life's journey,
the sisters God called home way too soon,
and for all the sisters I have yet to meet,
this book is for you.

A sister can be your best friend
or your worst enemy.
If she is your worst enemy,
chances are pretty good
that one of you broke the rules. . . .

Contents

Liz's Note

If you don't understand how a woman
could both love her sister dearly
and want to wring her neck
at the same time,
then you were probably an only child.

LINDA SUNSHINE, EDITOR AND AUTHOR

With three sisters and three daughters, I've learned a thing or two about being a sister and having sisters. I'm no relationship expert, but I *am* an expert sister. I love everything about sisterhood, and I can't imagine not having grown up in a home where there was always someone to talk to late at night, to watch a movie with, to laugh or cry with, or to agonize with over school, friends, boys, parents, or whatever drama was taking place. I firmly believe that no woman should grow up without at least one sister. While this isn't always possible, most women who have no sisters will undoubtedly find a best friend they call "sister." (See Rule #77 "All women are your sisters.")

Since my sisters and I are all speaking to one another and always have been, I'm so surprised when I hear a woman say that she's not speaking to her sister. When I probe for a reason, it's usually because one of them broke one of the Sister Rules.

I've been recording the Sister Rules silently in my mind since my girls were old enough to annoy one another. I've tried to instill in them the value of having sisters, and how lucky they are that they each have a sister to share life with. It's true that I didn't fully appreciate my sisters until I was older, but I wanted my girls to appreciate one another while they were still young.

When I heard them breaking one of the Sister Rules, I'd tell them so. "Megan, you just broke a Sister Rule," or "Kaitlyn, Sister Rule #13 says never to call your sister ugly," or "Kristen, just remember your Sister Rules. You can teach your sister a thing or two." When they were young, it worked. Kids take "rules" very seriously. But as they got older, I started to hear, "You're making that up! There's no such rule book, Mom!"

Oh, yes, there is. . . .

Growing Up
with Sisters

Rule #1

Don't call your sister names.

"Stop calling me names, you cheese head!"

MICHELLE TANNER, *FULL HOUSE*

Rule #2

If you're going to break Rule #1, make sure you do it when nobody else is around.

You wouldn't want anyone else calling your sister a [fill in the blank], would you? Sure, she's your sister and you can call her anything you want to (well, not really), but if someone else hears you and takes that as permission to call her a name too, you'll be very offended (being the good sister that you are).

So only break Rule #1 if you have to (and you don't usually have to), but make sure there are no other ears around. Better yet, do your name-calling only in your head.

Rule #3

Don't pull your sister's hair.

She might pull your hair back, and then you both could end up bald.

Rule #4

Don't be a space invader.

Give your sister plenty of personal space, unless she is in need of a hug. Then, by all means, invade. . . .

Rule #5

Share your stuff with your sister.

This doesn't mean you have to share everything. No hairbrushes, no toothbrushes (gross and unhealthy), no new sweaters, and definitely no FAVORITE denim jackets. These things are off limits and could prove unhealthy.

Rule #6

Don't expect your sister to share everything.

We are *all* allowed to keep some things just for just us.

Rule #7

Don't borrow your sister's clothes without asking.

"Best thing about having a sister: sharing clothes. Worst thing about having a sister: sharing clothes."
KAITLYN RUSSO, MIDDLE SISTER

Rule #8

Don't ask to borrow brand-new clothes at all.

At least, not until they have been worn by your sister twice.

Rule #9

If you do borrow your sister's clothes,
don't share them with your friends.
You may never get them back.

Rule #10

If you break Rule #9 and don't get them
back, think "replacement cost."

"If your sister is in a tearing hurry to
go out and cannot catch your eye,
she's wearing your best sweater."

PAM BROWN, AUTHOR AND POET

Rule #11

**If you stain borrowed clothes,
wash them before you give them back.**

Actually, wash them before you give them back,
even if you didn't stain them.

Rule #12

**Don't even *think* about touching
your sister's stuff.**

Unless, of course, you asked her permission,
and she heard you, and you heard her say yes.
Not you *thought* you heard her say yes, but
you actually *did* hear her say yes. Wait,
perhaps you should get a witness.

Rule #13

Never, *ever* call your sister ugly.

Chances are pretty good she looks a lot like you. If not, she might look like your mom, and if she breaks Rule #17 and tells your mom, then you're essentially calling your mom ugly, too. Things could get ugly.

> **"Your sister is the only creature on earth who shares your heritage, history, environment, DNA, bone structure, and contempt for stupid Aunt Gertie."**
>
> LINDA SUNSHINE, EDITOR AND AUTHOR

Rule #14

You break it, you bought it.

When you're in your sister's room, or even if you share a room, remember to treat her things the way you would treat expensive breakables in a store. (You can avoid breaking her things by following Rule #12.)

Rule #15

If you don't share a room, no visiting your sister's room when she isn't home.

Rule #16

**Don't make faces at your sister,
unless you are trying to get her to laugh.**

Rule #17

**When your sister says or does
something that annoys you,
don't say, "I'm telling Mom."**

This will only make her mad and will annoy
your mother (who has great hearing, especially
when she hears the "I'm telling Mom!" screech).
Try to work things out. If they don't work out,
try ignoring her. Easy to say, hard to do, but not
completely impossible.

Rule #18

**Never tell your sister to "shut up."
Instead, say, "Be quiet."**

"Shut up" is the start of a fight. "Be quiet" can
have the same effect, but not start a fight with
quite the same intensity.

Rule #19

**If your sister doesn't want to hear what
you're saying, shut up—er, I mean, be quiet.**

Rule #20

If your mom's in a bad mood, give your sister the "Mom's in a bad mood" warning.

This is great bonding moment for sisters. Avoid Mom at all costs and get along with one another.

Rule #21

If your sister is having trouble with homework, help her out if it's a subject you're good in.

You can always catch your favorite show later, but you can't always catch a sister when she's falling or failing.

Rule #22

Don't try to upstage your sister.

The only time you should play the "drama queen" is when you're trying out for the school play. Hard to believe, I know, but not everything is about you. Give your sister her time in the spotlight.

Rule #23

Don't play the cry baby.

That is to say, crying over every little thing—the "small stuff"—all the time. Unless, of course, you're 3 or under. This is the only time it is acceptable.

Rule #24

Don't ever say,
"Mom likes you best."

Might be true, but it has nothing to do with your sister. So don't blame her.

Rule #25

Don't take pleasure in your sister's pain.

When one of my sisters was getting yelled at, I always felt bad for her—even if it was because she was being mean to me. So refer to Rule #26, and have empathy.

Rule #26

Don't laugh if your sister falls down.

Bite your tongue, if you have to, to stop yourself from laughing. Break this rule only if your sister laughs first. But be forewarned: even if you only laugh once she's started laughing, she might get mad just the same.

Rule #27

Keep your sister's secrets
(but first, refer to Rule #28)

**"There's a special kind of freedom sisters enjoy.
Freedom to share innermost thoughts,
to ask a favor, to show their true feelings.
The freedom to simply be themselves."**

ANONYMOUS

Rule #28

Don't tell on your sister.

If it's just "small stuff." Most of it is. (See Rule #29.)

Rule #29

Do tell on your sister.

If the situation is serious and it's something you *know* is too big for you to handle alone, better to have your sister hate you for a while than to have NO sister.

Rule #30

Always play fair.

No cheating. If you're playing a board game and you're losing, no tipping the board over!

Rule #31

When you beat your sister at a game, don't be a sore winner.

Avoid saying, "Hah, YOU LOSE!" (Even if you know she tried to cheat.)

Rule #32

When your sister beats you, don't be a sore loser.

Don't say, "You cheated!" (Especially if you know she didn't.)

Rule #33

If you both made the mess, you both clean it up.

It's not fair to leave the job to just one of you. Excuses like "I have to do my homework" or "I have to do my hair" just don't cut it. Your sister is *not* your maid—she's your sister.

Rule #34

Don't be a "mother" to your little sister.

Believe me, one is enough. Little sisters don't like to be babied by older sisters, even if they are the "baby" of the family.

**"Big sisters are the crabgrass
in the lawn of life."***

LINUS, PEANUTS

**Maybe to Linus. He was, after all, just a brother.
Big sisters eventually grow into beautiful, loving women.
Crabgrass? Nah. Roses? Maybe . . .*

Rule #35

Don't get even.

If, by chance, your sister breaks a rule and you have the opportunity to get even, don't. Letting it go not only makes for good karma, it makes you a good person . . . and a good sister, despite the fact that you might have a sister who isn't so good at being a sister. And there isn't much you can do about that.

Rule #36

Don't be a "fun sucker."

In others words, don't take the fun out of everything. Sometimes sisters need to be silly.

Rule #37

Don't be a "bubble popper."

Don't downplay your sister's dreams. Instead, help her blow the bubbles, no matter how farfetched you think her dreams are. By the way, this rule includes bubble gum—it might get stuck in her hair.

Rule #38

Don't treat your sister like a chauffer.

If your sister has finally gotten her driver's license and you're still a few years away, don't expect her to drive you everywhere you want to go. If she does give you a ride (once in a while), give her money for gas (once in a while).

Rule #39

Always remember that older sisters _don't_ know everything, and younger sisters _do_ know something.

Older sisters usually can't help themselves with this one. They think that just because they were born first and started school first that they are smarter. Younger sisters catch up quickly, though, and after elementary school, everyone's pretty much on even turf.

Rule #40

Never talk behind your sister's back.

You know she'll find out one way or another. And it's rude.

**"To find out a girl's faults,
praise her to her girlfriends."***

BEN FRANKLIN

Obviously Ben didn't know that real sisters don't tell.

Rule #41

**If you tell your sister something
that you don't want anyone else to know,
make sure she is aware that it's a secret.**

Just in case, remind her twice that you are telling
her this in confidence—once at the beginning
and once at the end. This way, she can't say she
didn't hear you.

Rule #42

Just in case your sister forgot to tell you that she didn't want anyone else to know what she told you, ask her if you can share a story before you share it.

Recounting a humiliating event or painful life lesson your sister experienced may grab you a laugh from friends or strangers, but first ask yourself if your sister would mind. Chances are, she would. So be sure to check with her first. If she says, "Over my dead body," keep it to yourself no matter how hard it might be not to repeat it, even if she didn't listen to Rule #41.

Rule #43

**Parents aren't perfect,
so don't take everything they say
about you or your sister at face value.**

If your parents say things like, "Why can't you be more like your sister?" or "Your sister is the pretty one/smart one/thin one, etc." don't hold it against your sister. Each person is unique and should never be compared with another. Remember that, even if your parents don't.

Rule #44

Forgive your sister her little bits of whatevers.

And we all have a lot of those.

Rule #45

If you're in a bad mood, don't take it out on your sister.

Rule #46

**If your sister is in a bad mood,
don't take it personally.**

Rule #47

**If your bad mood is caused by PMS,
warn your sister.**

I always like to give fair warning. I just say, "PMS-ing!"
Of course, other women know to steer clear. (Most
men just don't get it.) And don't bother trying to
cheer up your "afflicted" sister—when her hormones
adjust in a day or two, she'll be back to normal.

I've heard that some women don't have these
extreme mood swings. It's got something to do
with their "healthy" diet. If you're one of them,
don't rub it in.

Rule #48

Watch soaps together
and learn how *not* to behave.

They always have at least one evil twin sister, or one sister who is sleeping with her sister's husband while the poor sister who's husband is cheating on her is now lying in a coma because some guy her sister was dating turned into a crazed lunatic who is wanted in two other states . . . or is that two other soaps? Whatever. Watch them and learn what not to do.

Rule #49

Make sure to have a movie date with your sister.

At least once a month. Too busy? Then once every two months. Still too busy? See Rule #50.

Rule #50

Make sure you speak to your sister at least once a week.

And never let more than two weeks go by without picking up the phone.

Sisters
& Dating

"You see a lot of smart guys
with dumb women,
but you hardly ever see a smart woman
with a dumb guy."

ERICA JONG, AUTHOR AND POET

Rule #51

Remember, sisters are forever.

Boyfriends (and even some husbands) come and go.

Rule #52

No man is worth damaging a "forever relationship" over, so . . .

Rule #53

Never date your sister's boyfriend.

Rule #54

Never date your sister's boyfriend . . .
even if they have broken up.

Rule #55

Never date your sister's boyfriend . . .
even if they have broken up
and you have her permission.

Rule #56

If your sister breaks Rule #53 and dates
your ex-boyfriend, remember Rule #1
(No name calling), Rule #3 (Don't pull
her hair), and Rule #4 (Don't invade her
space, especially with your fist).

Rule #57

When you meet your sister's new boyfriend for the first time, don't go by first impressions.

Give her "new" guy a chance to prove himself. It may take a while for you to see what she sees. You may never see it, but at least you can say you tried to like him (but say this only to yourself). Same can be said of a good first impression—sometimes you find a wolf (or perhaps a dog) in sheep's clothing.

Rule #58

Tell your sister you dislike her boyfriend only after following Rule #57.

If you dislike your sister's "man of the hour," you might think it is better to play the waiting game. Maybe she will dump him, but maybe she won't. Don't wait. Speak up ASAP. Since love is blind, as the saying goes, maybe she can't see what you're seeing. Keep in mind, a good sister knows us better than anyone. It's better to tell your true feelings before she forms an emotional attachment. She may take a closer look at him and see him as you do. Then again, maybe not. If that's the case, see Rule #59.

Rule #59

If you tell your sister that you don't like her boyfriend, say it only once.

You can't keep harping on it. She might see something in him that you don't and end up marrying the guy! Then, the fact that you disliked him so much that you couldn't keep your mouth shut will always be a wedge between you. If you say it just once, it can be forgotten.

Important note: If your sister ends up in divorce court after marrying the guy you couldn't stand, see Rule #75 (Never say, "I told you so.").

Rule #60

If your sister tells you she doesn't like your boyfriend, don't get mad at her.

Instead, consider what she has to say. She might have a good reason. If she breaks Rule #59, however, you are permitted to get mad.

Rule #61

If your sister thinks her life is over
because she doesn't have a boyfriend,
assure her that she doesn't need
one to be complete.

"A woman must not depend upon the protection
of man, but must be taught to protect herself."

SUSAN B. ANTHONY (1820–1906)
LEADER OF THE WOMAN-SUFFRAGE MOVEMENT

Rule #62

If you make plans with your sister, don't cancel.

Except in the case of extreme emergencies. Emergencies do not include "That cute guy finally asked me out, do you mind if we skip?" This is only an acceptable excuse if you haven't had a date in a very long time, and I mean a very long time, and even then, you can only use it once.

Rule #63

Don't set your sister up on blind dates, unless she asks.

You might think that guy you just met would be perfect for your sister, but don't tell him about your sister until you tell your sister about him. If she's interested, go for it.

Rule #64

If your sister sets you up on blind date, and you don't like the guy, don't blame her.

She tried.

Rule #65

If your boyfriend doesn't like your sister, think about getting a new boyfriend.

There is definitely something wrong with him if he can't see all the things that make your sister great.

Sisterly Advice & Honesty

Rule #66

No advice is better than bad advice.

Not to mention that sometimes, we just want someone to listen.

Rule #67

When telling your sister the truth, don't be too blunt.

Always try to be gentle.

Rule #68

**If your sister has a serious issue
that you can't help her with,
encourage her to seek professional advice.**

The key word is "encourage." You can't force her.
Just continue to be a part of her life anyway you can.
Keep encouraging her—and always offer to drive.

Rule #69

**If your sister is lacking motivation,
help her get motivated.**

Be her cheerleader and remind her of Rule #70.
"You can do anything! Yes, YOU CAN!"

Rule #70

If your sister is lacking courage
to change herself or her life,
teach her how to be brave.

Rule #71

If your sister is lacking faith,
give her some of yours.

It just might plant a seed and sprout some hope.

Rule #72

If your sister doesn't ask for advice, don't give it.

Just listen and bite your tongue.

Rule #73

If you break Rule #72, don't get mad at your sister for not taking your advice.

She didn't ask for it anyway.

Only dogs get mad.
THERESA KILLMAN, MOTHER

Rule #74

If your sister asks for your advice but doesn't take it, don't rub her face in it if things go wrong.

In other words, no saying, "I told you so." (See Rule #75.)

Rule #75

Never tell your sister "I told you so."

It's nice to be right, but she knows you told her and she knows she didn't listen. No need to rub it in.

Rule #76

Don't tell your sister what she wants to hear, tell her the truth.

If your sister can't depend on you to be honest with her, who can she depend on?

> "Best thing about having a sister:
> Someone to tell you like it is.
> Worst thing about having a sister:
> Someone to tell you like it is."
>
> LIZ

Sisters by Heart

"Chance made us sisters,
hearts made us friends."

UNKNOWN

"Chance made us friends,
hearts made us sisters."

LIZ

Rule #77

All women are your sisters, or at the very least have the potential to become one.

You can never have too many sisters or too many "Special Delivery Sisters." By this I mean the ones that God forgot to give us at birth, and we met along the way. Always have room for one more.

Rule #78

All women are born equal.

Each of us comes into this world naked . . . some of us get to wear beautiful layettes while others must wear hand-me-downs. But underneath it all . . . we are still naked.

Rule #79

Support your sisters by voting.

Many brave women fought long and hard for women to win the right to vote. Even if you can't exercise your body, exercise your right to vote. Unlike some exercises I've tried, voting takes only a few minutes.

> "There never will be complete equality until women themselves help to make laws and elect lawmakers."
>
> SUSAN B. ANTHONY

Rule #80

Avoid discussing politics with your sister unless you support the same political party.

If you must break this rule, try to respect each other's views. Agree to disagree. Unless of course you happen to be running for office in which case your sister should keep her views to herself. Likewise, if your sister is running for office, support her or keep quiet.

Rule #81

Do something good for all women.

Why? Refer to Rule #77. Support at least one issue that concerns women's rights and/or health. Join something or do something that can benefit all of us. For example, fight breast cancer or be an advocate for battered women. Whether it is through volunteering your time or simply making a donation to your favorite women's foundation, just do it. The help you give may save a life (it could be your own or that of a close sister or a sister you just haven't yet met).

Rule #82

**You can do anything your sister can do,
and she can do anything you can do.**

There is nothing you cannot learn. One person
is not necessarily smarter or more talented than
another, just perhaps more motivated.

Working Sisters & Stay-at-Home Sisters

Rule #83

All mothers, stay-at-home moms or not,
are working mothers.

Rule #84

If you have the luxury to be a stay-at-home
mom, or if you do it despite your struggles
to make ends meet, don't look down
on moms who work.

Some women have no other choice. They must work
to put food on the table. Some women don't need to
work for food, but have a variety of other reasons for
making that choice. Whatever the case may be, don't
judge your working sisters.

Rule #85

If you're a working-outside-the-home mom, don't take advantage of stay-at-home moms.

Sure, it's okay to ask for favors in an emergency, but don't make it a habit. Yes, your sister loves you and wants to help when she can, but don't make the mistake of thinking that just because she's at home, she can drop everything to save you in a pinch all the time.

Rule #86

If you find yourself asking for favors all the time ("Can you pick up my daughter from school? the game? etc.) and your sister hasn't yet complained, think about compensation.

This doesn't have to be about money. Perhaps you can take her kids for a weekend or an outing occasionally. Giving her some free time will mean a lot to her. A basket of fruit as a way of thanks is nice too. At least it lets her know her help is appreciated.

Rule #87

Keep in mind that we are all doing the best we can or the best we know how.

And it may not be the best as you define it, but it is her definition that counts for her.

Rule #88

If you think your sister is doing it wrong, don't tell her she's doing it wrong.

First you must remember Rule #72 ("Never give advice unless asked"). Just give a gentle hint by saying, "I don't know if it will help you, but this is what I did."

Sisters
Visiting Sisters

Rule #89

When you go out with your sister, treat once in a while.

Even if your sister has a million dollars in her checking account that she doesn't know what to do with and always offers to pick up the tab, don't let her get away with it. If you really can't afford to treat even once, you can make her an inexpensive home-cooked meal.

Rule #90

If you are invited to your sister's house for dinner, help anyway you can— even if she says she doesn't need your help.

My younger sister didn't agree with this rule—she feels that sometimes people just want their guests to relax. First, sisters are not guests. But I will say this: offer at least three times, with the last time not just asking but arising from your chair and making a good faith effort to help. If she still insists on doing it all herself, start thinking "she wants to be the martyr today." Then by all means, let her!

Rule #91

Don't take over your sister's kitchen.

Even if you think your sister lacks finesse in the kitchen and you're a master chef, fight the urge to take charge of the meal. Unless asked, don't start adding salt to the sauce, salt burns wounds.

Rule #92

Don't expect your sister to wait on you.

You're not a guest, you're a sister.

Rule #93

**If you need something,
get up and get it yourself.**

Rule #94

**Make sure you make the bed
in the morning.**

There is no maid service at your sister's house,
and after all it's a house, not a hotel.

Rule #95

If you're staying with your sister longer than a day and your sister has been serving you breakfast, lunch, and dinner, offer to do the cooking at least once or twice.

If you can't cook, take her out for dinner.

Rule #96

If you're staying with your sister as long as a week, buy groceries.

Don't expect her to stock your favorite premium coffee (especially if she is tea drinker) and those expensive muffins you love for breakfast. Make sure that you stock it in her pantry yourself . . . or be happy with the kids' PopTarts.

Rule #97

Treat your sister's home
the way she treats it.

If your sister is neat, be extra neat. If she is messy, mess things up a bit. . . . Just kidding, even if your sister is a slob, you still have to be neat. No need to add to the mess.

Rule #98

When staying at your sister's home,
try to go by her body clock.

If she stays up late, stay up with her, even if you're an early bird. Better to stay up late with her than wake her up early by pitter-pattering around.

Rule #99

**If you must move out of state,
try to stay in the same time zone
as your sister.**

One of my sisters moved clear across the country. She's in the Pacific Time zone, and here I am in the Eastern Time zone. This makes it more difficult to keep up with each other. I am by nature an early riser, up and about by 5 a.m., and to do this, I must be asleep by 10 p.m. the latest. When I get home from work, she's still hard at work. When she's making dinner, I'm getting ready for bed. So keeping in touch requires planning before picking up the phone.

Sisters with Children & Sisters with None

"My husband and I are either going
to buy a dog or have a kid
we can't decide whether to ruin our carpet
or ruin our lives."

RITA RUDNER, COMEDIENNE

Rule #100

**If your sister has kids,
don't reprimand them in front of her.**

Leave the disciplining up to her. If she doesn't say
anything, see Rule #104.

Rule #101

**Never say anything bad about your sister's
children even if they are the most
[pick your adjective here]
unruly, impolite, snotty, horrible, brats
who ever breathed the same air as you.**

Believe me, she knows. And if she doesn't know,
telling her that she is deluding herself isn't helpful,
only hurtful.

Rule #102

If you don't have any children of your own, offer to baby-sit once in a while.

Yes, even if they're bratty.

Rule #103

Take your sister's kids to a movie or out to lunch.

Not only will this give your sister a much-needed break, it will also give you some time to bond with your nieces and/or nephews.

Rule #104

Don't criticize your sister
for the way she is raising her children.

We are all doing the best we can, doing what we think is right.

Rule #105

Don't impose your personal beliefs
on your sister's children.

For instance, if you believe in eternal damnation for telling a white lie, and your sister believes there is no hell, don't mention it to her kids. You will not only scare the hell out of them, but you will make your sister mad as hell in the process.

Rule #106

If you have kids but your sister doesn't, don't expect her to baby-sit for your kids all the time.

Remember, your sister has a life, too.

Rule #107

If you have kids, but your sister doesn't, don't make her feel like she doesn't know the first thing about motherhood.

Even if you think it's true.

Rule #108

If your sister tries to give you
advice on raising your kids,
but doesn't have any of her own,
listen to her anyway.

She just may have some good ideas.

Sisters &
Body Image

"Inside me lives a skinny woman
crying to get out. . . .
But I can usually shut her up with cookies."

ANONYMOUS

Rule #109

If you haven't seen your sister in a while and she's put on weight, don't mention it.

Everyone owns at least one mirror and we all know what we look like. We can feel it when our clothes are a little tighter than they used to be and we know it when we're buying clothes that are a size or two larger. No need to state the obvious. Pretend you don't notice. Look into her eyes and you will see her heart is the same as it ever was, and that's all that counts.

Rule #110

**If you know your sister is dieting
(even if you think she's "fine" as is),
don't be a saboteur.**

You might think that everyone needs chocolate, but
right now your sister doesn't. Don't bring it over.

Rule #111

Never give up on your sister's diet.

Always support her. If you must bring a dessert
to her house, make it one that's low in calories.

Rule #112

Don't give her any chocolate, not even if she begs.

Okay, maybe if she is begging—but only after she does so for five minutes or more. She is having a weak moment and may be counting on you to help her out. Seriously, why do you even have chocolate on your person when you know very well your sister is on a diet? Never mind that it is her two hundredth diet, the important thing is that she keeps trying.

Rule #113

**If you see your sister eating something that's not on her diet,
don't ask her, "Diet not working?"**

'Cause then you've said a mouthful she won't be able to swallow.

Rule #114

Never tell your sister not to eat something because she is on a diet.

Rule #115

**Don't say, "Wow, you look skinny,"
just to make her feel better.**

If it doesn't look like she lost weight, don't pretend that you think she did.

Rule #116

Be happy for her.

When you hear her saying that she lost a few pounds, be a cheerleader (even if it isn't noticeable just yet).

Married Sisters
& Single Sisters

"I never married because there was no need.
I have three pets at home which answer
the same purpose as a husband.
I have a dog which growls every morning,
a parrot which swears all afternoon,
and a cat that comes home late at night."

MARIE CORELLI (1855–1924), AUTHOR

Rule #117

If your sister is getting married, be happy for her.

"The problem with women is that
they get all worried and crazy about nothing,
and then they marry him."

CHER, AMERICAN ACTRESS AND SINGER

Rule #118

If you don't like your new brother-in-law, suck it up.

You should have said your piece months ago
(see Rule #58). Now there's nothing you can
say. Be nice to the new guy.

Rule #119

If you can't stand being in the same room with your brother-in-law, make plans for a girl's night out with your sister as often as possible.

You'll only have to deal with him on those have-to occasions like holidays and family celebrations.

Rule #120

If you suspect that your sister isn't crazy about your husband, don't force them to be together.

Make plans for just the two of you. Everyone can't like everyone. Don't expect your sister to like him just because you married him.

Rule #121

If you're newly married,
don't forget your sisters.

Sure the honeymoon isn't over (at least not for a year), and you want to breathe the same air as him all the time. But make sure you breathe the air with the girls, too. You will survive if you two love birds spend time apart.

Rule #122

If your sister is newly married,
don't hold it against her if she can't
make last-minute plans with you.

You can however remind her of Rule #121 if she *never* has the time.

Sisters
& Divorce

"Whatever women do
they must do twice as well as men
to be thought half as good.
Luckily this is not difficult.

CHARLOTTE WHITTON (1896–1975),
CANADIAN FEMINIST AND MAYOR
OF OTTAWA

Rule #123

Never say, "I told you so."

In case you forgot Rule #75, this is just a reminder!

Rule #124

Never say, "I always hated him because . . ."

You may have to take those words and try to stuff them back inside your mouth, which may of course cause severe choking . . . if they decide to try to work things out.

Rule #125

If they do try to work things out, see Rule #118.

You will have to be nice once again.

Rule #126

If he leaves her for another women, don't hunt him down and kill him.

And don't bother kicking him in the balls because he probably doesn't have any. Just be there for her.

Rule #127

Help your sister to see that her divorce isn't the end of the world.

She can make it on her own even if you have to pinpoint each road and rest stop for her.

Rule #128

Never date your sister's ex-husband.

This rule needs no explanation.

Rule #129

If you're the one going through the divorce, call your sisters often.

They will help you get through this. By yelling, screaming, and crying at all the right times. They know just what it is you need to hear. They always do.

"Is solace anywhere more comforting than in the arms of a sister?"

ALICE WALKER, AMERICAN AUTHOR
AND FEMINIST

Growing Old with Sisters

"Thirty-five is when you finally
get your head together
and your body starts falling apart."

CARYN LESCHEN, GRAPHIC ARTIST
AND COPYWRITER

Rule #130

Always call your sister the day before her birthday and ask her how old she is.

It may be the last chance she gets to say that magic number. Only 29, only 39, only 49 . . .

Rule #131

Always call your sister on her birthday, but don't ask her how old she is.

You called yesterday. You should know that today she is the big Three-O, Four-O, Five-O . . .

Rule #132

**Never call your sister collect
on her birthday.**

You'll never hear the end of it.

"I was at a hotel. I didn't know I could use the phone.
I was only 19. I thought it was like a payphone
and I didn't have a quarter. . ."

CAROL KILLMAN ROSENBERG, YOUNGEST SISTER

Rule #133

**Make sure you and your sisters
get your annual mammogram.**

Rule #134

If you think your sister is dressing too young for her age, tell her. . . but only once.

She shouldn't be wearing the same clothes as her daughter (or her mother, for that matter). If she doesn't listen to you, see Rule #73. You can mention it twice, but only if her hearing is starting to go.

Rule #135

If your sister tells you that you are
dressing too young for your age . . .
you probably are.

"I base most of my fashion sense
on what doesn't itch."

GILDA RADNER (1946–1989),
AMERICAN COMEDIENNE & ACTRESS

Rule #136

Only a few women can carry off butt-length hair after age 60.

If your sister tells you it's time to get a new look, then you know you're not one of them. She is probably right, so you can't be mad. My younger sister disagreed with this, but I stand by my opinion. If you really insist on wearing your hair butt-length, I respectfully insist that you wear it up when you're out in public, for reasons I'll keep to myself.

Rule #137

**Say nothing if your sister cannot stand
the laugh lines around her eyes and
has now opted to put an end to them
with Botox or a face lift.**

Even if you don't think she needs it . . . it's her choice.
Say nothing. Don't try to talk her out of it—again her
choice. It's not for everyone, and maybe not for you.
What you can do is make sure she has found a
reputable doctor.

Rule #138

Always point out your sister's chin hair.

As women age, all of a sudden it is quite possible for these little hairs to start sprouting up on their faces. If your sister tells you it's time for a wax—and you don't think so—first have your vision checked, and then when you go to buy that new pair of glasses, make the appointment for a wax the same day. You'll be glad you did (and so will your sister).

Rule #139

If your sister is afraid of the doctor, go with her.

Drive her if you have to. Just get her to go.

"Sisters are connected throughout their lives by a special bond. Whether they try to ignore it or not, for better or for worse, sisters remain sisters until death do them part."

BRIGID MCCONVILLE, FROM *SISTERS: LOVE AND CONFLICT WITHIN THE LIFELONG BOND*

Rule #140

**Let your sister turn down the heat
if she is getting hot flashes.**

If you're not into that just yet, remember you
can only take off so many clothes until you're
naked . . . but you can always keep layering
those sweaters.

Rule #141

**If your sister is now a grandmother,
refer to Rule #100 and Rule #101,
but replace "kids" with "grandchildren."**

Rule #142

If your sister is trying to get back into your life, let her in.

Perhaps she broke a rule or two, and you find that you're no longer on speaking terms. Life is short. Let her in—you just might be glad you did (before you lose the chance altogether).

Rule 143

There are exceptions to every rule.

Even this one.

Rule #144

Always forgive your sister.

There are NO exceptions to this rule (see Rule #143).

"If there ever comes a day
when we can't be together,
keep me in your heart,
I'll stay there forever."

WINNIE-THE-POOH

In Parting . . .

There you have it, some of the basic rules for getting along with sisters. I leave the next page partially blank for you to come up with some of your own, as my sisters and I have over the years. I once broke a rule and didn't call her on her birthday . . . but she wasn't in the same time zone that day . . . and I was trying to stay awake until 10 when I knew I would be able to talk to her, and accidentally fell asleep. (But I did call her the day before.) I still haven't heard the end of it. So I came up with a new rule: If your sister breaks a rule, you are allowed to taunt her about for only six months. Seemed fair to me. . . . She agreed, but added: and once a year thereafter.

So for the mothers who want to give this book to their daughters . . . and sisters . . . feel free to come up with a couple of your own.

Rule

_____

_____

_____

_____

_____

Rule

_____

_____

_____

_____

_____

Rule #

_____

_____

_____

_____

_____

Rule #

_____

_____

_____

_____

_____

To my dearest sister, _____

I have to tell you how really, really sorry
I am for _____

_____.

I realize I have broken Sister Rule #_____
and Sister Rule #_____ and perhaps even
Sister Rule #_____.

I hope that you can find it in your heart
to forgive me (please see Rule #144).

I love you forever and always.

Your loving sister,

_____

Afterword

Most of these rules have always existed; just been unspoken. Some of them may seem a little silly, but upon reading them you'll find yourself nodding your head in agreement because you know they are true—they are there in your heart, with your sister(s), where they have always been. That is, until now, because sometimes some of us need to be reminded of how things are *supposed* to be.

If you're not speaking to your sister, pick her up a copy of this book and send it to her. Keep a copy for yourself, and get back to being sisters. Life is too short to go through it without one another. And if you're a mother of daughters, get them started young . . . let them know what the rules are.

Let's all play fair—it's the only way.

About the Author

Elizabeth Killman Russo, aka Liz, considers herself to be an expert at being a sister, since she herself has three beautiful sisters—Maryanne, Maureen, and Carol—each with their own unique perspective on the world. Despite this, they all manage to maintain that sisterly love and bond toward one another . . . well, most of the time. Elizabeth has also been lucky enough to have been blessed with two brothers, Jimmy and Michael. Both older, but certainly not wiser than she—but that is for another book.

Elizabeth is an artistic and a creative individual with lots of great ideas, this book being just one of them. The words *creative* and *brilliant* have been bantered around in the same sentence when some describe her, although she would never describe herself that way. She enjoys spending her free time creating poems, paintings, short stories, and designing centerpieces and other works of art. She is mother to Megan, Kaitlyn, and Kristen—three beautiful girls with beautiful hearts and many talents. Now that her daughters are grown, Liz is considering relocating to a warmer climate; however, she currently resides in New York, where winters can be brutal.

www.ingramcontent.com/pod-product-compliance
Lightning Source LLC
Chambersburg PA
CBHW031340040426
42443CB00006B/410